BOOK OF CAT NAMES

Amorous Alley Cats

Finicky Felines

Tender Tabbies

Cantankerous Kitties

& Tony Tomcats

SIMON JEANS

 Sterling Publishing Co., Inc.   New York

Library of Congress Cataloging-in-Publication Data

Jeans, Simon.
   Book of cat names / Simon Jeans ; [illustrations by Sophie
Blackall].
      p.   cm.
   Includes bibliographical references and index.
   ISBN 0-8069-8541-0
   1. Cats—Names.   I. Title.
SF442.4.J43   1992
636.8′088′7—dc20   91-39291
                                                                    CIP

Produced by The Watermark Press
Sydney, Australia
Design and Typesetting by Susie Stubbs
Cartoons reproduced by the kind permission
of The New Yorker Magazine, Inc.

10   9   8   7   6   5   4   3   2   1

First published in the United States in 1992
by Sterling Publishing Company, Inc.
387 Park Avenue South, New York, N.Y. 10016
Originally published in Australia and
© 1992 by The Watermark Press, Sydney, Australia
Additional drawings © 1992 by Sophie Blackall
Distributed in Canada by Sterling Publishing
% Canadian Manda Group, P.O. Box 920, Station U
Toronto, Ontario, Canada M8Z 5P9
Manufactured in the United States of America
All rights reserved

Sterling ISBN 0-8069-8541-0

Introduction

History, literature, sport and Hollywood are rich in cat characters, and in this slim volume we have included the names of all sorts of cats. The selection of names is, of course, arbitrary and concentrates on the historic, legendary and literary aspects of feline nomenclature rather than just amassing a huge list of names. If we have left out one of your favorites, do not give up hope. The omission is probably through lack of space and has nothing to do with suitability for inclusion. The editors are already anticipating an avalanche of letters offering names of legendary cats which we have overlooked, favorite names which should have been included, and tales of derring-do by our feline friends which remain unrecorded. We shall accept all your suggestions with good grace and, if this first collection proves as popular as we anticipate, we may consider a second book.

"But when she got there, the cupboard was bare, and so the poor dog had none."

Drawing by M. Twohy; © 1990 The New Yorker Magazine, Inc.

A

ABIGAIL   A dignified name for a mature cat. The diminutive, Abby, would suit a playful kitten perfectly.

ABRAHAM   "No matter how much cats fight, there always seem to be plenty of kittens." —Abraham Lincoln (1809-1865)

ADAM   A great name for the first cat you acquire. Also good if your cat likes to sit in the garden.

ADELAIDE   This name originates from an old German word meaning "nobility," so is most commonly bestowed on cats of the more stately breeds. This name can easily be shortened to Addy.

ADLAI   Adlai Stevenson once said, "It is in the nature of cats to do a certain amount of unescorted roaming."So perhaps you could name your roving cat Adlai.

AESOP   Sixth-century storyteller and collector of fables, particularly about animals. His characters are often stealthy or sly, knowing how to save their skins without offending those in charge.

AGATHA   A sleuth cat named after the prolific author of detective novels, Dame Agatha Christie. One of her books adapted for the stage, *The Mousetrap*, has run continuously in London for nearly 40 years.

AGNES   If she's particularly graceful, name your cat for Agnes de Mille.

AJAX   Ajax the Greater was the King of Salamis, renowned for his great physical size and bravery. A good name for a courageous cat. Also perfect for the cleanliness-conscious cat.

AKBAR   Akbar the Great, Emperor of the Mogul Dynasty, 1556-1605. He came to power at the age of 13 and greatly extended the empire through military genius. For the rags-to-riches cat.

ALBA   Meaning "dawn of day" in Spanish, and recalls the name of a famous painting by Goya of the Duchess of Alba, who was supposedly his mistress. This is a lovely name for the puss who is as pretty as a picture.

ALBERT   A traditional name which is now considered dated. If your cat is a bit plump, name him after the lead character in the cartoon show, "Fat Albert," narrated by Bill Cosby.

ALFIE   Short for Alfred, this short and snappy form implies a comfortable, pipe-and-slippers sort of a cat.

ALICE   The classic children's tale by Lewis Carroll, *Alice's Adventures in Wonderland*. In *Through the Looking-Glass*, Alice falls asleep playing with black and white kittens and ends her dream journey grasping the Red Queen, "shaking her into a kitten."

ALLEGRA   Or, if you prefer, Allegro. This was the name given to Byron's daughter. In music parlance it means "lightly, quickly" and thus describes perfectly a lively, playful cat.

AMBER   This translucent yellow stone is actually fossilized tree resin. Name your lovely golden kitten for it.

AMY   This simple name has famous connections. Amy was the youngest of the four *Little Women* written about by Louisa May Alcott. Dickens' gentle heroine in *Little Dorrit* was also called Amy. It would be most acceptable

THE BOOK OF CAT NAMES

for the family pet who is of no particular breed.

ANASTASIA   Derived from the Greek word for "resurrection," this name would be appropriate for kittens born around Easter. Also perfect for the cat born in Russia of royal parents.

ANGELA   From Latin and Greek words meaning "angel" and "messenger," respectively. Both, however, seem unlikely roles for the average cat, a factor which probably contributes to the use of the pet name, Angie.

ANNABEL   First noted in Scotland, but probably a corruption of "Amabel" from the Latin "amabilis," meaning lovable. For the affectionate puss.

ANTOINETTE   In France the name Antoinette has led to a few pet names, the most popular for cats being Toi and Toy.

ANTONIA   In Portugal and Spain the version of this name is Antonina, hence the very popular diminutive Nina. It will often be given to talkative cats with sensuous tendencies.

ANTONY   Antony the Abbot is the patron saint of domestic animals (and also patron saint of skin diseases!) his name day is January 17th.

ARCHIBALD   This name is common in Scottish households. Meaning "truly bold," it is particularly suited to reddish cats of strong temperament.

ARETHA   Aretha Franklin, "Queen of Soul." Give your cat this name if she can hit those high notes.

ARETHUSA Greek legend has it that the river-god Alpheus fell in love with the nymph Arethusa. She fled to Ortygia and was

turned into a fountain. Alpheus then flowed into the sea and rose in Ortygia and so was united with his beloved. Good names for an amorous cat or a pair of lovers

ARIA   Meaning "air," in music jargon, it usually suggests a piece extracted from a longer work. For a kitten or cat who is a chip off the old block.

ARIEL   This name is most suitable for a male cat of good breeding. A Hebrew name meaning "lion of God," Ariel is also a satellite of Uranus and appears in literature as a rebel angel in Milton's *Paradise Lost* and as an "ayrie spirit" in Shakespeare's *The Tempest*.

ARISTOTLE   A Greek philosopher (c.384-322 BC), he is remembered particularly for his work on logic and causality. A learned, serious cat would be proud of this name.

ARNOLD   Good for the thick-necked muscular cat with a hint of a foreign accent — your very own Mr. Universe.

ASPASIA   Considered to be a high-sounding name, it was used more than a century ago as a pleasant change from the Marias and Ellens of that time. Aspasia, meaning "welcome," was abbreviated to Spash by country folk.

ASTER   Aster means star and is also the name of a genus of flowers which includes the Michaelmas daisy. There is a variety known as the China aster, perhaps a name for an oriental cat.

ASTRAEA   Or more simply spelled Astrea, is a serene name for a cat. She was a goddess who dwelt on earth during the Golden Age, and her name means justice and innocence. But when evil entered the world, she was drawn up to the heavens to join the constellation of Virgo.

ATTICUS   The gentle hero of Harper Lee's classic novel *To Kill A Mockingbird*. For the intelligent Abyssinian cat.

AUGUSTA   For the Romans this name was a mark of majesty. It means "sacred" and "venerable" and was originally a title given to the women close to the Roman emperor. Short forms are Gus and Gussie.

AUGUSTUS   The male version of Augusta and the name given to Gaius Octavius, the first Roman emperor.

AYESHA   The title of a novel by Sir Henry Rider
           Haggard. It is a perfect name for an exotic
           cat.

B

BABE   Brought up to attract the richest and most
           distinguished men in America, Babe
           Cushing was one of three sisters known as
           the "fabulous Cushing sisters." For the
           stylish feline who sets the trends.

BABY   The pet tiger belonging to Katharine
           Hepburn's aunt in the film *Bringing Up
           Baby*.

BAGGINS   Bilbo Baggins was the hero of *The Hobbit* by
           J.R.R. Tolkien.

BAGHEERA   The panther in Rudyard Kipling's *The
           Jungle Book*. For the black cat who prowls in
           the garden like it was his very own jungle.

BALLOU   In the film *Cat Ballou*, Jane Fonda plays
           the title role which is a shortening

of her character's full name, Catherine Ballou.

BARBARELLA   From the sixties film of the same name, again starring Jane Fonda. Only for the way-out cat with silvery fur who is not desexed.

BARDOT   Brigitte, the "Sex Kitten" of the fifties. For the pouting prancing pet.

BARNABY   The first person to bear this name was the Apostle, his name in Aramaic meaning "son of exhortation." Dickens probably had more to do with the popularization of the name than that devout Cypriot.

BARNEY   Fred Flintstone's neighbor and bowling partner. A great name if your cat's a bit of a throwback to the Stone Age.

BASHOH   An ideal name for a wandering cat, after the itinerant Japanese poet Matsuo Bashoh.

BASIL   Yet another name with majestic overtones, this one means "kingly" in the original Greek. It probably doesn't mean anything like this to watchers of the TV series "Fawlty Towers," familiar with the antics of John Cleese as Basil Fawlty.

BAST, PASHT   The Egyptian goddess of love had the head of a cat and the body of a woman. The Egyptians had great respect for cats and when one died the owner shaved off his eyebrows.

BEATRICE   Also Beatrix, both meaning "bestower of blessings." And there are many diminutives: Bea, Bee, Beat, Beatty, Trix and Trixie.

BEATTY   Warren Beatty is reported to have been a rat catcher prior to his career in the movies. We'll say no more.

BEELZEBUB   In Milton's *Paradise Lost*, Beelzebub is one of the fallen angels. He is also a devil. For the cat with hypnotic green eyes.

BELLE, BELLA   "Lovely" and "beautiful" in just about anyone's language.

BERLIOZ   *See* DUCHESS

BERNIE   Suitable for a wise and home-loving cat, as the namesake is St. Bernard, who was renowned for his wisdom.

BERTHA   From the Old German word for "bright," Bertha was the name of Charlemagne's mother, acknowledged as a great beauty. For the larger varieties there is also Big Bertha.

BINGO   Like "Snap!" a cry of delight and enthusiasm, and a word to be called out loudly. A winning name.

BLACKBERRY   In Sussex, in England, a cat born just after Michaelmas (September 29th), which is the end of the blackberry season, is called a blackberry cat and considered to be mischievous.

BLANCHE   From the French "blanc," meaning white, a pretty name for a white cat.

BLATHERSKITE   And Zoroaster: Mark Twain used these tongue-twisters to help his children's pronunciation.

BLAZE   The name given to a white star on a horse's forehead. For the cat with a distinctive white marking on its face.

BLODWIN   A clumsy-sounding word of Welsh origin.

BLONDIE   The famous wife of Dagwood Bumstead from the comic strip of the same name. Also, the name of an American pop band, Blondie, fronted by Deborah Harry, would suit the "sex, drugs and rock 'n roll" type cat.

BLOSSOM   From the Old English "blostura," one who is lovely and full of promise.

BOLLINGER   A classy name for a champagne cat.

BONIFACE   In the Restoration comedy by Farquhar, *Beaux' Stratagem* (1707), this is the name of a jovial innkeeper, and has since become a generic name for innkeepers. Suitable for the bon viveur.

BONNIE and CLYDE   The famous gangsters played in the Hollywood film by Faye Dunaway and Warren Beatty. For a mischievous pair.

BORGIA   Son of Pope Alexander VI, Cesare Borgia
          terrorized central Italy during the late 15th
          century, murdered his elder brother and
          forced his sister into four political mar-
          riages. A good name for a true fiend.

BORIS   From an old Slav word meaning "fight,"
          Boris is a Russian name that has become
          popular in many other countries as well. It
          will apply well to those cats with a pugna-
          cious streak, or Russian blood.

BRAHMS   Johannes Brahms (1833-97) was a German
          composer in the tradition of Beethoven and
          a leader of the Romantic-Classical school.
          For the cat with a musical ear.

BRANDY   An ardent spirit distilled from wine or
          grapes and a name which denotes color.

BRODERICK   Crawford, a Hollywood tough guy of
          the 1940s and 1950s. Strictly for the
          hardbitten cat.

BRONTË   Wonderful for the dreamy cat who enjoys a
          good tramp on the moors, and a good
          companion to Heathcliff.

BUMBLE   For the clumsy kitten or cat who does not
          land on its feet.

BUMSTEAD   The harassed husband. *See* BLONDIE

BUNDY   Bundaberg Rum, yet another name derived from alcohol. This one is for the cat who claims his milk has been spiked, again.

BUTCHKIN   General Butchkin is the name of one of Doris Lessing's cats.

BUTTONS   The sunny personality of Buttons the cat brightened the dull domesticity of Cinderella's life. Very suitable for an affectionate kitchen companion.

BYTE   For the cat with megabytes of personality and charm.

C

CAGNEY   Warner Bros. moved James Cagney's date of birth forward five years to 1904, to exploit his baby-faced appearance. For the kitten that never grows up.

CALICO   Resembling calico material, spotted.

CANUTE   Danish sovereign who ruled England from
          1016 to 1035. Best known for his experi-
          ment to control the tide. For the cat with
          great faith in his own powers.

CAPONE   Alphonse "Scarface" Capone (1899-1947),
          the notorious Chicago gangster. This would
          be a good name for your brawling alley cat
          who's been in a fight or ten, especially if it
          shows.

CAPRICE   A tendency to change one's mind without adequate or apparent motive, ideal for those cats who scamper around the house in a world of their own.

CARBON   A copycat.

CARSON   For the pioneering type of cat who recalls the roving frontiersman Kit Carson.

CASANOVA   Giovanni Jacopo, the Italian whose legendary lovemaking made his name famous throughout the continent. Nowadays the name evokes a numbers game involving sexual conquests.

CASPAR   A salty sea-cat in tales of old, perhaps with Russian ties. For that rare cat that likes water.

CELESTE   A regal name for a somewhat ponderous feline, especially if it displays remarkable feats of memory as in the elephantine character from *Babar* by Jean de Brunhoff.

CHALKY   An affectionate name for a white and dusty cat, it could be paired with Cheese.

CHAN   After Charley Chan, the Asian-American sleuth. For a snoopy cat. A white alley cat named Charley Chan inherited his Missouri mistress' entire estate in 1978, including a three-bedroom house, a pet cemetery and valuable antiques.

CHAPLIN   Charlie. For the "little tramp" who walks off the street into your life and makes you laugh.

CHARLESTON   Originally an African-American dance, this became *the* dance of the 1920s. For the cat who is light on his feet and loves to dance.

CHARLIE, CHARLEY   The diminutive of Charles, a name used by royalty for many years. Kings and princes of France, Spain, Sweden, Hungary and England have borne this name, including, of course, the current Prince of Wales.

CHARIVARI   A French term for a mock serenade, usually after a wedding, made with the banging of pots and pans, kettles and the like. For the cat who likes to serenade you to the accompaniment of trash can lids.

CHARO   When you chuck your kitty under the chin, don't you ever get the urge to say "Cootchee, Cootchee?"

CHEECH, CHONG   The comedy duo, best for a pair; one small with pep and nerve, the other an aged spaced-out hippy.

CHELSEA   Could be named after the New York hotel patronized by artists and pop stars, or after the fashionable London suburb. Only for the cosmopolitan cat.

CHESHIRE   For the pet with a huge grin that brings to mind the Cheshire Cat in Lewis Carroll's *Alice's Adventures in Wonderland*.

CHIANG   From Chiang Kai-Shek (1887-1975), a Chinese soldier and politician who com-

manded Chinese armed forces during the Second World War. For the truculent alley cat, perhaps.

CHICO/CHICA   Meaning boy and girl, respectively, in Spanish, these would be ideal names for a pair of cats of both sexes.

CHIP and DALE   The lovable chipmunks from Walt Disney. Perfect for an audacious pair.

CHLOE   From the Greek, meaning "a green shoot," it was a title given to Demeter, the goddess of crops and fruit. For cats who like lending a paw or two at gardening time.

CHOCOLATE   For a tough brown cat with a soft middle.

CHRISTIE   Agatha, prolific mystery writer. *See* AGATHA

CHRYSOBERYL   The chrysoberyl, or cat's eye, is a yellowish-green stone said to have magic powers, and to protect the wearer from witchcraft. For the lucky cat with eyes to match.

CLARENCE   The cross-eyed lion in the 1960s TV series "Daktari," about an animal hospital in

Africa. For the cat who sees two of everything.

CLARIBEL   A more sophisticated alternative to Clare, from the Latin clarus (clear) and bellus (beautiful). This would be the perfect name for an elegant white cat.

CLAUDE   After the limping, stuttering Roman emperor, Claudius. For the cat who is not as quick on its feet as it used to be. Or perhaps for the famous composer, Claude Depussy?!

CLEOPATRA   The Queen of Egypt who bewitched Antony and Caesar. For the elegant black cat with a striking profile.

CLOVER   A four-legged charm.

CLYTIE   In ancient mythology Clytie was an ocean nymph in love with Apollo, the glorious and powerful god of the sun. When he deserted her, the gods in pity changed her into a sunflower, which continued to follow his course in the sky throughout the day.

COCOA, COFFEE   Both of these are pretty, if slightly predictable names for your dark brown cats.

COMET   *See* HALLEY

CONSTANTIA   Meaning constant, unchanging. It was very popular in Russia, where, as in France, it was associated with royalty. According to Cato, Constantia also means "cautious." For the regal cat with a sense of decorum.

CORDELIA   For the faithful feline. Cordelia was the youngest of King Lear's three daughters, and the only one that loved him.

CORINNA, CORA, KORA   These attractive names derive from Kore, one of many titles given to Persephone. Rowena is another name, and so is Cora, each of them pleasant in sound and association.

CRESCENDO   Musical term for gradually getting louder. For the cat who begins an increasingly deafening plaint of miaows around dinnertime.

CRUNCHY   A must for the chocolate and honeycomb-colored cat.

CYCLOPS   For the one-eyed feline.

CYNTHIA   A name used poetically to denote the moon.

D

DAEDALUS   According to Greek mythology, Daedalus made wings for himself and flew from Crete across the Archipelago; his son Icarus flew with him, the sun melting the wax which fastened the wings, so he fell into the sea. Good names for an inventive, daring duo. *See* ICARUS

DAISY   From the Anglo-Saxon "day's eye," for the daisy's petals which close over with the approach of night.

DAISY MAE   Abner's girlfriend in the Al Capp cartoons; a good name for a cat who likes to stop and smell the flowers.

DALE   *See* CHIP

DALLAS   The epitome of glitz and gossip, and the television series everyone loved to hate. Just the title for a cat with enormous self-esteem and padded shoulders.

DARIUS   King of the Persians (c. 558-486 BC). For that regal Persian in your house.

DELILAH   Good for one of a pair, with Samson.

DENIS, DENNIS   This name originated from Dionysus, the protector of wine, who was worshipped at the grape-harvest festivals. Dennis is the usual Irish spelling.

DESMOND   A sensible name suggesting a smart cat who always lands on its feet. Can be readily shortened to the more affectionate Des.

DIANA   An ancient Roman goddess commonly regarded as a moon-goddess, and also goddess of hunting. She once enraged the gods by assuming the form of a cat. For the beautiful cat who hunts at night.

DINAH   If your cat's always in the kitchen, name her Dinah.

DIVA   For the cat who makes caterwauling an art form, especially at night with an unwilling audience.

DIXIE   For cool cats from Southern states.

DIZZY   A good name for a cult cat suited to the Bebop era of jazz. If your tom can play the trumpet then look no further.

DONNA   Name your cat for Donna Summer if she loves to love ya.

DORA   The name of a cat belonging to Annabel Bool. The cat's full name was Adorabool. Believe us.

DORIC   A pleasant-sounding word conveying dignity and style. Doric is one of three Grecian orders of architecture, (Doric, Ionic and Corinthian), and is the simplest, oldest and strongest.

DORIS   Maurice and Doris. Perfect for a boy/girl pair.

DORSEY   After Tommy Dorsey, the big-band leader. Does your cat like to hang out at night with his or her friends, creating a "big-band" racket?

DOT/DOTTY   Short for Dorothy and appropriate for a scatty cat.

DUCHESS   A dignified white Angora cat featured in the Disney film *The Aristocats*, with kittens called Maria (who wants to be a primadonna), Toulouse (who wants to be a painter) and Berlioz (who wants to be a composer).

DUSTY   Literally meaning "strewn with dust," an affectionate name reflecting darkish coloring. A Texan tabby named Dusty is claimed to have had 420 kittens.

E

EARL   For the puss in aristocratic boots.

EARTHA   Eartha Kitty, a wonderful name for the cat with a sexy, sultry purr.

EBONY   Intense blackness, with an exotic air, like the hard blackwood native to Ceylon and Mauritius. Lovely for one of a pair, where colors contrast; Ebony and Ivory.

ECHO   In Roman mythology, Echo was a nymph whose love for Narcissus was unrequited, so she pined away until only her voice was left. A suitable name for a cat who shadows a companion.

EDDY   Mary Baker Eddy (1821-1910) was an American who founded the Christian Science movement, promoting spiritual healing of physical problems. For a mind-over-matter cat.

ELBA   Napoleon's island of exile, for the cat whose territory is limited.

ELIOT   Author of *Old Possum's Book of Practical Cats*, T.S. Eliot's work has been popularized by the hugely successful musical *Cats* (1981).

ELIZA   For Eliza Doolittle, the heroine from *My Fair Lady*. An apt name if you're constantly trying to improve your cat's manners.

ELLA   From an ancient Germanic word meaning "all," this name was revived by the Victorians but immortalized by that jazz great, Ella Fitzgerald.

ELLIE MAE   The ingenuous blonde of the Clampett clan in "The Beverly Hillbillies."

ELSA   The Old German for "noble maiden," Elsa has undergone its greatest revival as a name for cats with Joy Adamson's tale of her beloved lion Elsa in the book *Born Free*.

EMMA   Emma Hamilton was Lord Nelson's mistress. If your cat has a tom as a friend who is blind in one eye and is missing his front right paw, then Emma is right for her.

ERRATA   A good name for the kitten who you were once determined not to adopt.

F

FANNY   After Fanny Brice, a great comedienne in the thirties, for your comic cat.

FANTASIA   Inspire musical appreciation in your cat by naming it after this 1940 animated Disney film, which gives a visual interpretation of compositions by Tchaikovsky and others.

FAROUK   Farouk I (1920-65) came to the Egyptian throne in 1936. His increasingly hedonistic, extravagant life-style led to dissatisfaction among his subjects, and he was deposed in 1952. This name would suit an exotic, flamboyant and very fat cat.

FAT CAT   The only name for a cat in the public service.

FATHER GOTTO The wise old cat who presided over all the others in the fairy tale *The Colony of Cats* by Andrew Lang.

FAUNA One of the three sprites in Disney's version of *Sleeping Beauty*. If your cat protects the house with a little magic, here's a good name for her. *See* FLORA, MERIWETHER

FAUNTLEROY For most people this name has but one association, that of the little American boy in the Victorian novel who won all hearts. But it has medieval Anglo-French origins. "Faunt" was derived from "infant," "leroy" from "le roi," the king.

FEIFFER For the witty cat, from the well-known U.S. cartoonist. Would also suit a sultry, sensual cat who likes to lie on top of pianos as actress Michelle (P)feiffer does in *The Fabulous Baker Boys*.

FELIS Our domestic cats come from the genus *Felis catus*.

FELIX Felix is a Latin word meaning happy and is the name of the animated feline star of countless silent movies of the Twenties. Would suit a cat with huge eyes and an unblinking stare.

FLASH   For the cat with the superhero streak.

FLOPSY, MOPSY   After Beatrix Potter's rabbits in *The Tale of Peter Rabbit*.

FLORA   One of three sprites in Disney's version of *Sleeping Beauty*. *See* FAUNA, MERIWETHER

FLUFF/FLUFFY   For your Angora kitten.

FOSS   This famous pet of 19th-century humorist Edward Lear lived to the age of 17. Lear immortalized him in a series of sketches.

FRACAS   An ideal name for a troublesome cat who is the cause of many mishaps and squabbles.

FRECKLE   If your pet is spotted or has markings on his nose, call him by this affectionate name.

FREYA, FREJYA   The pagan Scandinavian goddess of love and fertility whose chariot was said to have been drawn by cats.

FRISBEE   For the light-footed beach-loving cat.

FUM   Fum is an unusual name for a golden cat. In Chinese legend, Fum was the phoenix born in the Sun's halo.

G

GABIN   Jean, a famous French movie star. For the
           sleek cat who charms the birds out of the
           trees.

GABLE   Clark, King of Hollywood. For the fashion-
           able feline who makes all the female cats in
           the neighborhood swoon (and doesn't give a
           damn).

GALAHAD   Reputedly the purest of all King Arthur's
           Knights of the Round Table. For the cat
           with fur like freshly fallen snow.

GANYMEDE   In Greek mythology the cupbearer of
           Zeus, a youthful male beauty. In Shake-
           speare's *As You Like It*, Rosalind disguises
           herself as a man and takes the name. So if
           your tom is good-looking, then this is
           perfect.

GARBO   Greta, the late and great movie star. For the
           smoky Persians or sultry Siamese who just
           want to be alone.

GARFIELD   The lasagne-loving superstar owned by the
           hapless Jon.

GAYLORD   From Middle English, meaning "lively" or "gay." For the cat who knows how to enjoy life.

GENEVA   The city in Switzerland, which is usually associated with the Red Cross, this name is also connected with the alcohol gin. The Old French genèvre, or juniper berry is used to flavor gin.

GEORGE   This name comes from the Greek for "tiller of the ground" or "farmer." For a country cat.

GERDA   An original choice for a white cat. Gerda is found in Scandinavian mythology, the daughter of the Frost Giant Gymir. Gerda was so beautiful that the brightness of her white arms illuminated both air and sea.

GHOST   An elusive or illusive cat.

GIACONDA   La Giaconda, Mona Lisa, for the enigmatic cat who looks as if she's swallowed the canary.

GIB   Short for Gilbert, an ancient name for a cat, especially a tomcat, and which later came to mean a castrated tomcat. Chaucer wrote of "Gibbe, our Cat," and Shakespeare wrote in *Henry IV*, "as melancholy as a gib cat."

GIBB   A cat hauled up in the notorious English witch trials of the 17th century. According to trial records, it was said that Gibb had the ability to speak. So if your cat manages more than meow...

GILBERT   This would also suit one of a pair of cats who sing for their supper; the other would be Sullivan, of course. *See* GIB

GINGER   A common name, referring to the color of the coat, though C.S. Lewis thought

differently. The *Chronicles of Narnia* ends with *The Last Battle*, in which Ginger the cat becomes puppet of the devil.

GIZA   The suburb of Cairo where the most famous sphinx is situated. The sphinx has a lion's body and a human head, usually that of a pharaoh.

GLORIA   There have been many famous women with this name. Name your cat for Archie Bunker's daughter, for Gloria Swanson, or for the hurricane of 1985 which devastated New York's Long Island!

GODIVA   For a chocolate-colored cat.

GODOT   From Beckett's renowned play *Waiting for Godot*, written in the tradition of the theatre of the absurd. For the intangible cat.

GODZILLA   If your kitten's a little terror, then name if after Godzilla, a film monster (awakened by an H-bomb) who menaces Tokyo.

GOLDIE   For the companion who is worth his or her weight in gold.

GONZO   The lovable Muppet with a huge nose who conducts a choir of singing chickens. Also a form of journalism which specializes in the bizarre, as pioneered by American writer Hunter S. Thompson.

GOOLAGONG   If your cat shows promise with a ball of wool, then think of Evonne Cawley, née Goolagong, the first Aboriginal Australian to gain prominence in world tennis, winning the women's singles at Wimbledon in 1971 and 1980.

GRACIE   One half of the comedy duo, Burns and Allen. If your male cat's named George, here's a perfect name for his mate.

GREEDIGUT, GRIZZEL   17th-century familiars named in Hopkins' treatise *The Discovery of Witches*. He claimed that these were names "no mortal could invent."

GREYMALKIN, GRIMALKIN   An old cat, especially a witch's familiar.

GRINGO   The Mexican slang word for foreigner. For the cat who appears out-of-place.

GRISELDA, GRISEL   This name means a woman of exemplary patience and meekness. It comes from the story of Patient Grisel, the last tale in Boccaccio's *Decameron*. From there it was used by many other authors, including Chaucer, who tells of Grissell who endured the humiliations and cruelties inflicted upon her by her husband without so much as a murmur. They do not make cats like this.

GRIZZLE   This word has two meanings, to complain or whine, and also grey-haired. Sound like someone you know?

GRUNDY   "Solomon Grundy born on a Monday…" A good name for a cat with a short life expectancy.

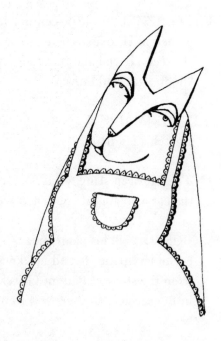

GUMMO   One of the Marx Brothers, or perhaps the pet who sticks to you.

GUSTAV   A dignified name, after Gustav Holst (1874-1934), composer of a nocturnal animal's dream music, *The Planets*. Also a name found frequently amongst Scandinavian royalty.

H

HALLEY   Halley's comet is named after the English astronomer (1656-1742). "Comet" comes from the Greek meaning "long-haired star," and has the additional connotations of speed and spectacle.

HAMADRYAD   The Hamadryads were nymphs who lived and died with the trees that they inhabited. As a tree is usually a safe harbor for cats who are being chased by dogs, this is an apt name for most varieties.

HAROLD   If your pet shows leadership qualities, this name of kings would spur him on to greater heights. An irreverent abbreviation would be Harry.

HARPER   *Harper's Bazaar*, the world-famous fashion magazine. This name would be perfect for the cat rarely known to stray very far beyond Fifth Avenue.

HARVARD   Cats love books as they make such a comfortable place to sleep or wash. A good name for a college cat.

HARVEY   If your cat is a cocktail of breeds, a wallbanger, or simply a tipsy mixed breed, then Harvey has all the right connotations.

HAZEL   If your feline friend fixes you with a big green-eyed stare, then this is the ideal appellation.

HEATHCLIFF   Cartoon cat of criminal propensities, or the brooding lover of Catherine from *Wuthering Heights*.

HECUBA   The Queen of Troy. According to legend, she clawed out the eyes of the King of Thrace, and was later transformed into a dog. Does your cat have an evil temper? If so you could threaten her with the same fate.

HEGEL   For the philosophic cat who likes to sit back and observe the wonders of the universe.

HENDRIX   Jimi was described by *Life* magazine as "a rock demigod," by the *New York Times* as the "black Elvis," and by John Lennon as the "Pied Piper of rock." A good name for a wild and groovy cat.

HERCULES   In legend, Hercules helped Jason find the Golden Fleece. The name has become synonymous with great strength and would be ideal for the muscular male.

HERMIONE   Famous British comedienne, for the kitty with refined diction.

HILDA   A Celtic British saint. Hilda sponsored Caedmon in his literary endeavors. Perfect name for the cat with sense enough not to park herself on your writing tablet.

HOCUS POCUS   Words uttered by a magician when he performs a trick that usually turns out to be a con job. For the devious cat who pulls the wool over your eyes.

HODGE   A plain country name, ages old, which probably derives from Roger. Would suit a no-nonsense cat.

HONEY   For the sweetest cat in all the world.

HOPE   One of the trio of Hope, Faith and Charity.
         If your kitten is a terror now, you can hope
         she'll grow out of it.

I

ICARUS   Icarus is, in Greek mythology, the man who
         defied his father Daedalus and flew too close
         to the sun, thereby melting the wax of his
         man-made wings, causing him to plummet
         into the sea.

IGNATZ   From the cartoon "Krazy Kat." Appropriate
         for the cat whose behavior is inexplicable.

IMELDA   A fitting name for the puss with a penchant
         for shoes.

INCA   A Peruvian cat would fit the bill.

INDIA   Name her after the subcontinent, or for the
         color of her fur which is as black as india
         ink.

INIGO · Inigo Jones revolutionized British architecture, adding Italian styles (such as the Queen's Chapel at St. James's Palace) to London's drab streets. Definitely a name for a sophisticat.

IRMA · Name your cat for *Irma la Douce*, if she likes to loiter on street corners late at night.

ISAAC · For the cat who attempts to defy the law of gravity.

ISIS · Goddess of ancient Egypt, wife of Osiris. A wonderful name for the helpful, faithful companion.

ISOLDE · *See* TRISTAN

J

JACK · A wonderfully simple name with many different connotations, such as Jack-in-the-box, Jack Frost, Jack the Ripper, Jack and Jill, Jack rabbit, Jack Horner, or any one of many famous men, a name to suit any cat.

JACKSON   General Stonewall, or after the artist,
Jackson Pollock, for that creative creature.

JACOB   Hebrew patriarch, who wrestled with an
angel. Watching your kittens tussle in play
may bring this name to mind.

JADE   Only for the cat with eyes of purest jade.

JARMARA   The name of a witch's familiar, traditionally
thought of as feline, belonging to a woman

seized by Matthew Hopkins, the notorious witch-finder, of 17th-century Britain.

JASPER   For Jasper Johns (b.1930) the American painter, or for the stone, which is usually red, yellow or brown.

JAZZ   For the syncopated feline who dances to his own rhythm.

JEEVES   P.G. Wodehouse's comic valet. If your cat has impeccable manners, this is the name.

JEMIMA   For an old duck of a cat.

JEREMIAH   Perfect name for a cat whose wailings seem to be eternal.

JEOFFRY   A pleasant name, with added pleasure if you recall Christopher Smart's lines from *Jubilate Agno* about his cat Jeoffry.
"For he counteracts the powers of darkness by his electrical skin and glaring eyes."

JINGO   Principal Head of State of Japan AD 360. Archaic but still a lively name. Not to be confused with "Jingoism," a peculiar British disease.

JOEY   Pal, as in the musical *Pal Joey*.

JONAH   Biblical hero, swallowed by a whale. For the
             cat whose fish-loving habits may get him
             into trouble.

JOSHUA   Biblical hero, conqueror of Jericho. If your
             cat's voice reminds you of a trumpet blast,
             Joshua may be a good name for him.

JOYCE   A popular girl's name in the mid 20th
             century, which can also be used for a male,
             perhaps in reference to the literary giant
             James Joyce, the author of *Ulysses*.

K

KARMA   In Buddhism/Hinduism, this is the unbro-
             ken sequence of cause and effect; a Sanskrit
             word meaning "action" or "sequence." The
             perfect name if you and your cat are on the
             same wavelength.

KELLOGG   For the flaky cat who loves his breakfast.

KENTUCKY   If your cat has some American ancestry
             or likes to gamble on the classic Kentucky

Derby, then this is ideal. Or, if your feline is as fast as a bullet and never misses the mark, Kentucky Pill is not so sweet slang for bullet.

KEROUAC   Jack Kerouac of course, favorite author of the "Beat Generation" and one hep cat.

KILKENNY   During the Irish rebellion, soldiers would tie two cats together by their tails and throw them across a line to fight. The obvious name for a tormented cat.

KINGSTON   If your feline's fur inclines towards dreadlocks and he listens to reggae, then name him after the capital of Jamaica.

KIR   A champagne cocktail. For the cat with blonde and red markings.

KLUTZ   Perfect name for the clumsy cat.

KORBUT   After Olga, for a flexible cat.

KOSHKA   A lovely sounding name for a mooching Muscovite mouser. It is, in fact, the Russian word for "cat."

KRAMER   From the film *Kramer vs. Kramer*. For the cat who's the center of a custody battle.

L

LEO   Leo is Latin for "lion." If your pet thinks he is King of the Jungle and has a ferocious miaow, then no other name will do.

LEONA   Hotelière and convicted felon. For the haughty cat with little concern for the little people.

LEONARDO If your cat has a natural creative flair or an enigmatic smile, then name him after the great Renaissance painter Leonardo da Vinci (1452-1519).

LEROY   From French origins "le roy" meaning "the king." The cooler cats will appreciate the name as immortalized by Jim Croce in the song *Bad, Bad Leroy Brown*.

LIBERTY   To the Romans the cat was a symbol of Liberty, to Americans the Statue of Liberty represents democratic freedom. For the emancipated cat.

LILY   In *Through the Looking-Glass* the Red Queen introduces Alice to "My precious Lily! My imperial kitten!" to which the Duchess

retorted "Imperial Fiddlesticks!" If you are lucky enough to have an imperial or even an imperious kitten, Lily could be an appropriate name.

LIVINGSTONE   I presume... The famous doctor who spent a lot of time in Africa, discovering places and documenting his travels. For the adventurous cat.

LIZINA   The kind young servant to a colony of cats who as a reward for her services was dipped in liquid gold, catching the eye of the young Prince who fell in love and married her. *See* FATHER GOTTO

LOLITA   A youthful temptress in the novel of the same name by Vladimir Nabokov. For the kitten-cat who seduces you from the start.

LOTHARIO   "Is this the haughty, gallant, gay Lothario?" Nicholas Rowe's famous seducer of women from *The Fair Penitent*. A name to live up to.

LOTTIE   Short for Charlotte, the resourceful spider in the delightful children's book later made into an animated film, *Charlotte's Web*.

LUCY, LUCILLE, LUCINDA, LUZ   These names are all derived from the Latin word *lux*, meaning "light." For those who light up your life. Lucille, perhaps after Lucille Ball, the red-headed comedienne from the "I Love Lucy" shows.

LUPINO   After Ida Lupino, famous Hollywood actress of the 1940s. For the glamorous cat.

LYNDA   Lynda Bird Johnson, elder daughter of L.B.J., and as the wife of Charles Robb, first lady of Virginia. For a Southern-born cat, with family connections.

LULU   Cartoon character. Perfect for the diminutive cat of any breed.

M

MABEL   A name derived from the Latin word "amabilis" meaning "lovable." Diminutive forms are Mab and Mabs.

MACAULAY   A distinguished name not to be used frivolously. Namesakes include Catherine, radical historian; Dame Rose, novelist and travel writer; and Thomas Babington, politician and historian.

MACHIAVELLI   With an obvious diminutive, this makes reference to Niccolò Machiavelli (1469-1527), the Italian political theorist and writer whose name has become synonymous with political intrigue. A cat with an evil streak, perhaps.

MAC/MACK   For the computer cat. Also an affectionate name for an older mouser, akin to mate or buddy.

McKENZIE   Sir Compton McKenzie was a Scottish
            author perhaps best known for his riotous
            book *Whisky Galore*. For the cat with a
            penchant for a kilt.

MADONNA   A contrary name, perhaps a much revered-
            cat who nevertheless shamelessly flaunts her
            sexuality.

MAE   The type of cat that might purr, "Come up
            and see me sometime." Definitely a bed-
            room type of cat.

MALFI   The desire of a widowed duchess to marry
            beneath her position is cruelly thwarted by
            her brothers in John Webster's *The Duchess
            of Malfi* (1614). For the pedigreed puss who
            lusts after the tabby down the road.

MAME   Lead character of the comic novel and
            Broadway musical. A good name for the pet
            who could coax the blues right out of the
            horn.

MANX   A tailless variety of cat.

MAO   After Mao Tse-Tung (1893-1976), a fearless
            swimmer and one of the founders of the
            Chinese Communist Party. For revolution-
            ary cats.

MARS   Roman god of war and the fourth planet from the sun. For a bellicose cat, a red cat, or one who's just from another planet.

MARTHA Sister of Lazarus and Mary Magdalene, Martha is the patron saint of housewives. Not a name for the liberated feline, but if your cat is somewhat old-fashioned, then Martha is a saintly name for her.

MATILDA Like Jemima, Matilda seems to be rather a haughty name. It was introduced by the Normans, and there were several queens of that name. It is a compound of "might," "strength," "battle" and "strife," a somewhat belligerent name.

MAUDRED Old-fashioned name for an old-fashioned cat.

MAXWELL Smart, Agent 86, from the sixties spy spoof series, "Get Smart." Ideal for a pair; Max and 99. Also the perfect name for a coffee-colored cat, after Elsa Maxwell, a Washington socialite.

MAZUMA Slang for money. Appropriate for an expensive, exotic cat.

MAZURKA After the Polish dance. A beautiful name for a long-furred foreign feline.

MEDUSA   To look at this cat might turn one to stone.

MEHITABEL   The name of a wise and sophisticated
little cat whose friend and confidant was a
cockroach named Archy.

MEL   Owner of Mel's Diner in the TV series
"Alice." Name your cat for Mel if he's fond
of greasy-spoon cuisine.

MERIWETHER   The third of three sprites in Walt
Disney's version of *Sleeping Beauty. See*
FAUNA, FLORA

MERRY   For your carefree, cheerful, convivial,
comical, carousing cat, especially if it has
entered your life at a festive time of year.

MERYL   Streep. For the versatile mouser who takes
on many and varied roles throughout her
life.

MEWSETTE   Star of a 1962 feature cartoon *Gay
Purr-ee* about a country cat who comes to
Paris and is kidnapped. Judy Garland's voice
was used for Mewsette.

MIKADO   A lovely name for an oriental mouser.
Brings to mind the much-loved opera written by Gilbert and Sullivan in 1885.

MILLAMANT   Congreve's Millamant in *The Way of the World* was one of the first champions of feminism. It was Millamant who said "A little disdain is not amiss; a little scorn is alluring," and how well that describes some little Abyssinian beauty.

MINERVA   The Roman goddess of wisdom.

MING   One of the most famous dynasties of China (1368-1644). For a fine porcelain cat.

MINNALOUSHE   The underworld connection again. This was a black cat immortalized by Irish poet W.B. Yeats, who was widely known to have been fascinated by the occult. This cat is described as "the nearest kin of the moon."

MIRANDA   The daughter of Prospero in Shakespeare's *The Tempest*. Her name means to be wondered at.

MISFIT   When no other name will do.

MISS PUSS   Dick Whittington's cat, otherwise known as Cat, from the fairy tale by Andrew Lang, *Dick Whittington and His Cat*. A memorial has been built in her memory on Highgate Hill, London.

MR. MAGOO   A short-sighted cartoon character who frequently bumped into things. A good name for a clumsy cat.

MR. TIBBS   Sidney Poitier's three Mr. Tibbs detective films made this name famous. If your feline friend is something of a sleuth, look no further.

MITZI   A popular name in Britain for the family mouser. Also appropriate for the cat with a touch of glamour, like Hollywood star Mitzi Gaynor.

MOCHA   A fine-quality coffee originally from Yemen, where the region known as Mocha is situated. Can denote a rich coffee/chocolate coloring.

MOHAWK   From the native name, one of a tribe of North American Indians. Ideal for the cat with spiky fur.

MOLOTOV   Originally the name of a Bolshevik. Today, it is best known as an explosive cocktail. Pick a volatile cat to suit.

MONROE   Marilyn. For the blonde bombshell who believes that diamonds are a cat's best friend.

MOPSY   *See* FLOPSY

MORGAN   Perhaps after Morgan le Fay, queen of
           Avalon and King Arthur's half-sister, who
           tried ambivalently to kill and cure Arthur.
           Morgan revealed to Arthur, through a magic
           draught,the intrigues of his wife Guinevere
           and Sir Lancelot. For the cat who hides its
           claws.

MORTICIA   The Gothic wife of Gomez in the cult sixties
           TV series "The Addams Family," about a
           family from the "dark" side who try to
           integrate into normal suburban life. Only
           for the black feline.

MOWCHER   A Dickensian character, Miss Mowcher was
           the diminutive hairdresser employed by
           Strenforth and introduced to David
           Copperfield. She was quick-witted, observ-
           ant and sharp.

MOZART   Wolfgang Amadeus. A perfect name for the
           genius cat. As Mozart was not the most
           demure of people, the abbreviation of his
           first name to Wolfie should not offend.

MUFFIN, MUFFINS   A very popular name with
           children, it would suit a roundly shaped
           mouser.

MYSOUFF   The pet cat of 19th-century French writer Alexandre Dumas. The cat was reputed to have had psychic powers.

N

NANCY   When Nancy Reagan became First Lady this name leaped to prominence. It is not known whether the cat in the White House was equally well-dressed and confident.

NEFERTITI   The Egyptian queen with the famous profile. For cats whose image deserves to be recorded in plaster.

NELLIE   The gossipy housekeeper in *Wuthering Heights* who recounts the tale of Heathcliff and Cathy. For the homey cat who loves to lie on the hearth rug by the fire.

NICHOLAS   The last tsar of Russia. If your cat wanders, name him after the last of the Romanoffs.

NIJINSKY   Vaslav (1890-1950), one of the most famous Russian dancers and choreographers of all

time. Alas, he went mad in 1917 and the world was the poorer. An excellent name for any lithe and graceful cat.

NILE   Cats were worshipped in ancient Egypt. Name your cat for the life-giver of Egyptian civilization.

NOEL   Is your cat not at all courageous? Name him for Noël Coward. Also a good name for a kitten given as a gift on Christmas.

NORA   Nora Charles, wife of Nick. Sleuth of film fame, from the Thin Man series. For the witty, elegant, and snoopy cat.

O

O'MALLEY The Alley Cat in *The Aristocrats*, who introduces himself to Duchess as Abraham de Lacy Giuseppe Tracy Thomas, in an attempt to impress. A smarmy animal.

OCTAVIA A classic Roman name, perhaps the most famous Octavia being Marc Antony's abandoned wife whose charms faded in comparison to Cleopatra's.

OLAF Name of several distinguished Scandinavian kings.

OLIVER "Please sir, can I have some more?" A famous line from the film *Oliver!*, adapted from the book by Charles Dickens. For the hungry and lonely cat forced into a life of petty theft to survive.

OMEGA The last letter in the Greek alphabet and a name that signifies the last in a series.

ONASSIS Short and slick; a good name for a ship's cat.

ORLANDO Orlando the Marmalade Cat is the hero of a classic series of picture books by Kathleen

Hale, first published in 1938. Orlando and his wife Grace are accompanied by kittens Pansy the tortoiseshell, the white Blanche, and coal black Tinkle.

ORSON   According to fable, Orson and his twin brother Valentine, were born in a wood near Orléans, where Orson was taken by a bear and suckled with her cubs. He later became the terror of France, known as the Wild Man of the Forest. Orson Welles fans will be interested to know the origin of the name.

ORWELL   George Orwell once said that "All animals are equal, but some are more equal than others." For the cat who's a cut above the rest.

OSIRIS   Husband of Isis, and Egyptian god of the underworld. A mystical name for a serious cat.

OTTALINE   An amorous cat in memory of Lady Ottaline Morel, a literary figure who had many lovers.

OTTO   Prince Otto von Bismarck, if you prefer to use his full title. Use it for your pedigreed Prussian.

P

PATTI Name your cat for Patti LaBelle, American singer, if she has a distinctive voice and hairdo.

PEARL A rare and valued feline, especially apt for the maternal cat: Mother-of-Pearl.

PEBBLES Fred and Wilma's daughter from "The Flintstones." For the cat who tracks litter through the house.

PEDRO Emperor of Brazil. Perfect for the coffee-colored cat.

PEPPER For the speedy mouser with unusual markings or little black flecks through his fur.

PERCIVAL According to some versions, Percival, Knight of the Round Table, found the Holy Grail. A somewhat archaic name well suited to that Middle-Aged cat.

PERIWINKLE The greater and lesser periwinkle are evergreen trailing shrubs with light blue starry flowers. The name is also applied to small blue mollusks found on the seashore.

PERRY   Fred Perry was a tennis player and Pery or
               pirie is a pear-tree or a drink similar to
               cider, made from pear juice. Perry is also a
               diminutive of the Greek name Pericles.

PHARAOH   Literally "great house," so be sure of your
               feline's lineage before you bestow this title.

PHOEBE   Means "shining one," the name the ancient
               Greeks gave to the goddess of the moon.
               According to legend, Phoebe was a Titan,
               daughter of Heaven and Earth.

PHUKET   For the Siamese cat who takes its holidays at
               Club Med.

PIAF   French slang for "sparrow." Also the sur-
               name chosen by legendary singer, Edith
               Piaf, who was only 4 feet 10 inches tall. For
               the very small and fragile cat.

PICKLES   For the puss constantly getting into a jam.

PIERROT   An inspired name for a black and white cat,
               especially a very thin one, looking rather
               like a sad clown. If he had a mate, the obvi-
               ous name for her would be Pierette.

PIP   Short for Philip, as in Charles Dickens'
               character Philip Pirrip in *Great Expectations*.

PINKLE PURR *See* TATTOO

PITTI SING and **YUM YUMM**   Two of the three little maids from school from *The Mikado* by Gilbert and Sullivan.

PIXIE   A light-footed cat with magical presence.

PRINCE   This is a dignified name for a pedigreed cat. It would also suit the cat with a penchant for purple if named after pop superstar, Prince.

PUSHKIN   A lovely onomatopoeic moniker with distinctly Russian associations — Aleksandr

Pushkin was a distinguished writer of the 19th century.

PUSS   From the children's pantomime "Puss 'n Boots" and the nursery rhyme "Pussy Cat, Pussy Cat, where have you been?" "I've been to London to visit the Queen."

PYEWACKET   In the film *Bell, Book and Candle*, Kim Novak played a witch with a cat by this name. It was also one of the witch's familiar's names, as found in Matthew Hopkins' *Discovery of Witches* in 1647.

Q

QUEENIE   A very popular name that came into favor in the early years of Queen Victoria's reign. It became a tribute to the highest feminine qualities.

QUENTIN   San Quentin, the famous California prison. Does your cat constantly tear holes in the screens trying to get out? If he does, then here's a good name for him.

R

RALPH   A good name for a tomcat, especially one with red hair, after the character Ralph Malph in the TV serial "Happy Days."

RAMBO   A savage mouser would suit this name that has become synonymous with an image of a sweaty soldier of fortune.

RANDY   Common American nickname; vulgar adjective. You could name your cat after "Randy" Andy, Duke of York, or simply name him after the Randolphs of Virginia, descendants of Thomas Jefferson.

REGINA   Somewhat regal, as the name means queen, but it can be shortened to Reggie for that slow moving, languid cat.

RHAPSODY   Meaning a grandiloquent piece of music, this name would suit a cat who likes to do things on a grand scale. Also brings to mind the much-admired jazz concerto *Rhapsody in Blue* by George Gershwin.

RHUBARB   A popular choice for the family favorite. Could denote a rather ruddy coat. In

Rhubarb, an American film, made in 1951, an alley cat named Rhubarb inherits $30 million and a major league baseball club.

ROCHESTER   If your cat is large and dark or hides a secret, then name him after Charlotte Brontë's hero, Mr. Rochester, in *Jane Eyre*.

ROCKY   For a fighter who claws his way to the top.

ROCOCO   A lush style of decoration from 18th-century Europe, appropriate for a flamboyant feline.

RODDY   British child star, and later, American film actor. Known for his role in *How Green Was My Valley*, McDowell starred in many other fine films.

RODIN   The thinking person's cat.

ROLLS   Name your cat for the Rolls-Royce engine if he's got an engine that really purrs.

ROMEO   From Shakespeare's immortal *Romeo and Juliet*. The name has since developed connotations of insincere flattery and seduction, so if your cat is a heartbreaker, this name would suit.

ROMERO   Cesar, the often flamboyant Hollywood actor of the 1950s who played The Joker in the TV series, "Batman." For the cat who loves to play practical jokes.

ROXANNE   The meaning of this name, which is also found as Roxana and Roshana, is "dawn of day." She was one of Racine's heroines. The name has recently been revived and popularized as the title of both a movie and a song.

RUSTY   This is a very popular name, often denoting a reddish hue to a cat's fur.

S

SAFFRON   A spice used for its distinctive orange coloring, from the Arabic *zafaran*. An imaginative alternative for your orange cat.

SAGE   For a feline that is either greenish gray, like the healing herb, or for the cat who seems judiciously wise, or pretends to be.

SALAMI   An irreverent name for a sausage-shaped cat.

SAMBA An erotic Brazilian dance — only if your cat is a full-blooded, passionate Carioca.

SANTA Claws: a Christmas special.

SATCHMO Meaning Satchel Mouth, after the famous jazz trumpet player Louis "Satchmo" Armstrong. For a voracious but friendly cat.

SATHAN/SATAN A cat who appeared in the Chelmsford witchcraft trials of 1579. An appropriate name if your pet is black with pointy ears and tail.

SCIPIO To ensure that there is no disrespect to the noble Roman General, we should change the

spelling of this name to Skippio. For those who name their cats by sound rather than sense.

SCROOBIOUS PIP   From Edward Lear's poem — all the beasts in the world try to place a mysterious creature who insists its only name is Scroobious Pip. For that unique cat.

SEBASTIAN The elegant down-and-out hero of Waugh's *Brideshead Revisited*. Reminiscent of a golden, decadent time, your cat should have all the faded splendor of the English aristocracy.

SEKHMET This Egyptian goddess was the "Great Cat." Her influence is wholly good, and as one would expect, she is linked with the moon. A very special, awe-inspiring name.

SERGEANT TIBS   The cat in *101 Dalmatians* by Dodie Smith.

SERSA   If you prefer Xerxes to Ahasuerus, but feel that the spelling is likely to cause embarrassment, why not choose Sersa as a simpler version. It is quite a pretty name.

SEUSS   A tribute to the late author who created the wonderful *The Cat in the Hat*, and many other hilarious and dynamic children's books.

SHABBOTTEY   An amusing and interesting name for a cat. It comes originally from *Chat Botté* — the booted cat, "Puss 'n Boots" in fact.

SHADOW   For the blackest black cat who likes to follow you around.

SHERLOCK   After Sherlock Holmes, the famous British detective. If you have a pair of inquisitive kittens, consider calling them Holmes and Watson.

SHERRY   Originally, white wine made in Spain at Xeres or Sherris, now Jerez. Sherry is suitable for cats with a variety of colors, from the pale dry to smooth dark brown.

SHIRLEY   Originally a boy's name, it was popularized by Charlotte Brontë's *Shirley*. Also suitable for a cat with curls, after Shirley Temple Black, child star and later U.N. Ambassador.

SI and AM   The devious pair of Siamese cats in *Lady and the Tramp*, a Disney film.

SIBYL   Cats are mysterious, and so were the sibyls of Roman mythology. They were prophetesses who lived to a great age and who were models of female intellectual beauty.

SIMON   The oldest pet forms of this name are Symond, Symkyn and Simpkin. The tailor's cat in Beatrix Potter's *Tailor of Gloucester* was called Simpkin.

SINH   A cat with golden eyes that was worshipped in Burma by a sect of priests who believed it had oracular powers. Perfect for the Burmese pet.

SISTRUM   In ancient times this was a metal rattle, used especially in the worship of Isis. On the upper bend of the instrument there was usually a carving of a cat's head, often with a human face.

SISYPHUS   Mythical figure of Greek legend. Good name for a cat whose repetitive behavior appears to be futile.

SKINDLESHANKS   A railway cat made famous by T.S. Eliot. No train could leave without him.

SKITTLE   For the skittish kitten who often sends things flying.

SMARTY   For the cat with a high I.Q. who is sometimes a little big for his boots.

SNAGGLEPUSS   This skinny pink lion became a
popular TV cartoon figure. Exit stage left —
stage right even!

SNAP   Snap, crackle and pop! Ideal names for a
playful trio.

SNARK   From *The Hunting of the Snark* by Lewis
Carroll. Be sure your cat is bizarre enough

to compete with Carroll's mythological creature.

SOOTY and SWEEP   These teddy-bear puppets were created in the 1950s by Harry Corbett and are still favorites. Both would suit a black cat.

SOPHIA   A name recalling the voluptuous Italian actress Sophia Loren. Your feline would have to have an hourglass figure.

SORAYA   The name of the first wife of the late Shah of Iran. Soraya was sad, lonely and beautiful. A good name for an imperious Persian.

SORREL   For a bright chestnut-colored cat.

SPEED   *See* VALENTINE

SPHINX   The Egyptian Sphinx was a lion, usually with a pharoah's head, symbolizing royal power. This name would lend itself to a mysterious and powerful feline. *See* GIZA

SPIDER   For the long-legged cat.

STELLA   Means "star" in Latin. The name was originally coined by Sir Philip Sidney, who wrote sonnets and songs collectively titled

Astrophel and Stella. Also Stanley Kowalski's wife in *A Streetcar Named Desire*. Perfect for the cat who loves you even in your rattiest undershirt.

STEPHEN   After thriller writer Stephen King whose films include *Cat's Eye*, in which a cat becomes involved in some very bizarre situations.

STEVIE   "Oh I am a cat that likes to
Gallop about doing good."
But unfortunately Stevie Smith gave no name to the jolly good-natured creature described in her poem *The Galloping Cat*. Might we not then call a cat with such an agreeable disposition "Stevie?"

STYMIE   Character from "The Little Rascals." This would be good for the kitten who is a bit of a scamp, or whose behavior puzzles you.

SUNDAE   A treat for every day of the week.

SWEEP   *See* SOOTY

SYDNEY   Why not name your cat after this beautiful Australian city? One thing you can be certain of, Sydney will never be dull.

SYLVESTER   The black and white cartoon cat who splutters when he talks and who is forever tormenting the poor little canary Tweetiepie.

T

T'ANG   Dynasty of China (618-907). Well suited to the oriental breed.

TABASCO   The perfect name for a saucy cat with a red-hot temper.

TABITHA   The comfortable cat, as depicted by Beatrix Potter. Also for the famous feline who performs magic when she twitches her nose, as Tabitha does in the popular 1960s TV series, "Bewitched."

TAROT   If your cat has unexplainable powers and can foretell the future, name it after the tarot-card pack.

TATTERS and RAGGS   Apt names for a scraggly looking pair.

TATTOO   "Tattoo was the mother of Pinkle Purr,
A little black nothing of feet and fur;"
Christopher Milne, son of A.A. Milne, and
the model for Christopher Robin in the
Pooh books, recalling his favorite cat.

TEAZLE   In Sheridan's *The School for Scandal*, Lady
Teazle was a charming lovable coquette,
flirtatious but fundamentally faithful to a
husband twice her age.

TESS, TESSA   For the rags-to-riches (and back to rags
again) type of cat, after the beautiful heroine
in Thomas Hardy's novel *Tess of the
D'Urbervilles*.

THATCHER   Margaret Thatcher, British Prime
Minister, gained fame, originally, for de-
priving English children of their govern-
ment-subsidized milk. Name your cat for
her if she runs up large milk bills.

THOMASINA   Heroine of a novel by Paul Gallico,
later filmed as *Three Lives of Thomasina*, in
which the feline heroine recovers from three
crises, to the joy of her young mistress.

TIBBY   Short for Tibert, the cat who appeared in
Reynard the Fox. *See* TIBERT, TYBALT,
TYBERT

TIBERIUS An imposing name for an imposing creature. Can be shortened to the more friendly Tiber.

TIBERT, TYBALT, TYBERT The French form of Gilbert, this is a traditional name for cats. Tibert is the cat in *Reynard the Fox*, and Shakespeare uses the reference for his character in *Romeo and Juliet* — Mercutio addresses Tybalt as "a rat-catcher" and "Good King of Cats!" *See* GIB

TIDDLES From the old English slang to indulge, nurse and cherish. For those pampered pets.

TIGER Not only will this name refer to the markings on your cat, but he will also have a wild streak.

TIGGER The lovable but incorrigible tiger in *Winnie the Pooh* whose bounce and bravado get him into all sorts of scrapes. For the amiable and adventurous cat.

TIGGY Abbreviation of either TIGGER or TIGER.

TITANIA In Shakespeare's *A Midsummer Night's Dream*, Titania is the wife of Oberon and Queen of the fairies. For the bewitching cat who casts a spell over you.

TOLSTOY A distinguished name. Leo Tolstoy (1828-1910) was the world-famous Russian writer, whose well-known works include *War and Peace* and *Anna Karenina*.

TOM A male cat. The name was popularized by the world-famous Tom and Jerry cartoons, about a cat and mouse who are sometimes friends, usually enemies.

TONTO Co-star with Art Carney of *Harry and Tonto* (1974). A homeless New Yorker and his cat journey across America.

TONY Broadway's highest award. For the dramatic cat.

TOP CAT The famous television cartoon cat who lived in a garbage bin but is the most "tip top" and the king of the dump. Diminutive is T.C. or Top.

TORQUIL, SOMERLED It is sometimes very difficult to trace a name back to its first usage. Torquil and Somerled, very fine names, have long been considered as Scottish. Unusual and gracious.

TORTILLA A Mexican cat who adds a bit of spice to your life.

Drawing by M. Stevens; © 1991 The New Yorker Magazine, Inc.

TOSCANINI   Arturo Toscanini. Famous Italian con-
             ductor. Great for the cat who leads the
             feline chorus.

TOULOUSE   After the wonderful but tragic French
             painter Henri de Toulouse-Lautrec. *See*
             DUCHESS

TOWSER   Reputed by the *Guinness Book of Records* to be
             history's best mouser, catching an estimated
             28,899 mice during her lifetime, an average
             of 3 a day.

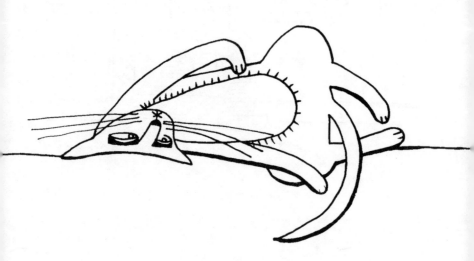

TREVOR Trev is the pet form. For the down-to-earth cat who takes life as it comes.

TRISTAN And Isolde. Classic medieval love poetry involving love potions, madness and fatal love. For the star-crossed feline lovers.

TUDOR The name of English sovereigns from Henry VII to Elizabeth I. Should only be bestowed upon cats with impeccably royal lineage.

TUTANKHAMEN The youngest of the Pharaoh kings to die, Tutankhamen was embalmed, in accordance with the ancient Egyptian custom. Easily shortened to the more manageable "Tut".

TWAIN Mark Twain's *Notebook* (1935), published posthumously, recalls the comment that "If man could be crossed with the cat it would improve man, but it would deteriorate the cat."

TWIGGY For the doe-eyed model cat who is as skinny as a rake.

TWITCHER Who but a cat could be called Twitcher? Jemmy Twitcher, the highwayman in Gay's *Beggar's Opera* was described as cunning and treacherous.

TYPHOON   The name for a tropical cyclone or hurricane of the western Pacific or the China Sea. Literally, from the Chinese for Great Wind — Tai Fung. For the little whirlwind who wreaks havoc in your house.

U

ULANOVA   The Russian ballerina Galina Ulanova. For your Russian Blue who is light on her toes.

URIEL   Uriel was one of the seven Old Testament Archangels, and according to Milton (in *Paradise Lost*) was the "Regent of the Sun," and "sharpest sighted spirit of all in heaven."

UTOPIA   A Latin essay by Sir T. More published in 1516 about the search for the best possible form of government. Today, it refers to absolute and ideal future. For the cat perfect in every way.

U NU   Burma's first Prime Minister after independence. A good name for a male Burmese.

V

VALENTINE   February 14th associations aside, *See* ORSON. Also one of Shakespeare's *Two Gentlemen of Verona*, whose serving-man is named Speed.

VALENTINO   For the hot Latin lover who has his pick of the felines on your street. Brings to mind Hollywood superstar and seducer Rudolph Valentino.

VARUNA   In Hindu mythology, Varuna was one of two virtuous sons of Aditi, the Earth Mother. A spirit of the night in the orbit of the moon. He appears as one riding on a sea monster, and from his exalted position orders the seasons and controls the rains.

VELVET   A fitting name for the Burmese pet with fur as soft as velvet.

VENUS   The Roman goddess of love and the second planet from the sun. For the great beauty with a place high in your affections.

VERONICA   Rich girl in "Archie" comics. This would be a good name for a brunette cat, and especially one who enjoys great rivalry with a blonde called Betty.

VESUVIUS   For the cat whose eruptions can be violent.

VIOLET   These lightweight flower names are suitable for cats, and generally pleasing. Violets are associated with shyness and modesty, the white ones with innocence, the purple ones with faithful love.

VIVALDI   Antonio (1675-1741). This name is in honor of the much-loved baroque composer who wrote the world-famous *Four Seasons*.

VOGUE The magazine. When no other name will do for your fashion-conscious feline who likes to strike a pose.

VOLTAIRE Pseudonym used by François-Marie Arouet (1694-1778), the famous French satirist, novelist, dramatist, poet and historian. For the cat who thumbs its nose at the establishment.

W

WAFFLE A cat without substance, but sweet nonetheless.Would be great for a cat with cross-hatched markings.

WARLOCK This name means "doing the work of the devil." Only if you are not afraid of things that go bump in the night.

WANDA Wanda Gag, the great author of children's books, particularly fond of cats.

WASHINGTON This name originally derives from the English village of the same name. It is more famous though through George, father of his country.

WENDY   A theatre name invented by James Barrie for one of the Darling children in *Peter Pan*. *See* NANA

WHISKERS, WHISKAS   For the cat with brand loyalty.

WHISKY   The "spirituous liquor" originally distilled in Ireland and Scotland. In rare usage, can also mean "light," "lively" and "flighty"; an apt descriptions of how one feels after a drop of whisky.

WHISPER   For the quiet, graceful cat who moves silently around the house.

WHITEY   Whitey Ford, baseball great, formerly of the New York Yankees. An obvious name for a cat of this color with good ball skills.

WILBUR   Very popular in the U.S.. Probably comes from the German words for "will" and "defense." For the tom who defends his territory.

WILFRED   Comes from the Anglo-Saxon words for "will" and "peace." The short form is Wilf.

WILMA   Wife of Fred and mother of Pebbles, the voice of reason in the Flintstone's Stone Age household.

WILLIAM   Charles Dickens called his cat William, but quickly changed its name to Williamina when it gave birth to kittens.

WILLOW   Although its origins are obscure, this word is associated with sorrow, as in weeping willow. It would suit a willowy and melancholy cat.

WINIFRED   Means "friend of peace." In the first-century AD, St. Winifred was beheaded because she refused to marry Prince Caradoc. The usual pet forms are Win, Winnie and Freda.

WINNIE   A homely name, and the nickname of wartime British politician, Winston Churchill. Also a great name for a cuddly pussycat that brings to mind Christopher Robin's Winnie the Pooh.

WONTON   Chinese dumpling, eaten with soup. A good name for your rotund pet.

WOODBINE   Earthy and wholesome sounding, it is the common name of wild honeysuckle. Use it for an untamed kitten.

X

XAVIER   Not after Francis Xavier, but Xavier Cugat. A good name for a remote musical cat.

XEROX   A good name for a copycat.

XERXES   The King of Persia, defeated at Salamis by Themistocles.

Y

YANKEE   New York baseball team, the "Bronx Bombers." If you have nine or ten cats, you could name them for the whole team!

YENTA   Wonderful name for the cat who can't mind her own business.

YIN and YANG   In Chinese philosophy, these are the two principles of the universe. One, Yin, represents the feminine, passive side, while the other, Yang, represents the active, assertive side. These would be great names for a pair of opposites.

YORIIE   Principal Head of State of Japan (1202-1204).

YUM YUMM   *See* PITTI SING

YVETTE   A sophisticated French name It would probably suit a Persian or other pampered breed.

Z

ZADOC   From Dryden's satire of *Absalom and Achitophel*. Zadoc was a priest whose "lowly mind advanced to David's grace."

ZELDA   Wife of F. Scott Fitzgerald. If you sometimes wish that your cat would move to Paris, here's the name for her.

ZEPHYR   Babar the elephant's little monkey friend was called Zephyr. Zephyr is also a soft gentle breeze.

ZIGGY   Cartoon character, or Ziggy Stardust, David Bowie's alter ego. For a cat who's alternately comical and musical.

ZINGARO   The Italian name for a gypsy. This name is for the cat who likes to travel in a caravan and who can predict the future with its crystal ball.

ZOE   From the Greek, meaning "life." For that "little bundle of joy," perhaps a new kitten.

ZOLA   Emile, the leading figure of the French school of naturalistic fiction during the 19th century.

ZULEIKA   Not only the fascinating Zuleika Dobson, but reputedly the name of Potiphar's wife who brought so much trouble to the innocent Joseph. The name is frequently found in Persian poetry, so it would be an appropriate name for a similar brand kitten.

Index

A

C

D

F